Merriam-Webster's
Ready *for* School Words

Merriam-Webster's

Ready *for* School Words

1,000 Words for Big Kids

By **Hannah Campbell**
Illustrated by **Sara Rhys**

Merriam-Webster kids

Contents

Foreword

"What's that?" the child asks, and so begins a lifelong exploration in language. At Merriam-Webster, we've devoted the past 180 years to exploring words, carrying on the legacy of the father of American dictionaries, Noah Webster, and spreading our love for words. What is it about words that we love so much?

Words are **magical**. Words can weave stories that introduce children to new people, take them to strange lands, and transport them to different times. They show us the world through the eyes of others.

Words are **fun**! As every comedian knows, words can tickle your funny bone and turn frowns upside down. As a child grows and acquires language skills, they learn to understand and appreciate word play and humor.

Words are **powerful**. Words can open minds and stir hearts. By naming ideas and emotions we come to understand them. At crucial times in history, words have brought change to the world.

Words matter.

When a child enters the world of *Merriam-Webster's Ready-for-School Words*, they'll be introduced to new words and meanings for things they encounter in their community and beyond. With this new vocabulary, they'll start school, and a lifetime of learning, with confidence.

The Editors at Merriam-Webster

Introduction

Dear Reader,

Look around the room you're in right now. How many things do you see? How many of them can you name? If you take this book outside, you'll see even more things, like plants, animals, people, or buildings. It's a big world out there—and everything in our world has a name!

Think of the word *hat*. Some hats keep your head warm when it's cold. Other hats help you stay cool on a sunny day. A hard hat protects a builder on a construction site, and a chef's hat keeps their hair away from food. They're all different, but hats all have one thing in common: they cover our heads. Learning new words helps you see the secret connections between all kinds of things.

The people you'll meet in this book also have many things in common, and plenty of things that make them unique. They have different kinds of families—some might even look like yours. You'll get to know these characters in everyday places such as home, school, or the park. And they'll take you to some exciting places, too! Everywhere they go, there will be new words to learn and connections to discover.

Words aren't just names for the things we see and do. Words bring us closer to our friends, families, and neighbors. They let us tell stories and jokes, or ask people for help when we need it. Words give us something to share with other people. For all the things that make us different, words can bring us together.

Happy reading!

Hannah Campbell

Meet the Main Characters

The Chen family

Ms. Chen, pilot

Grandma

Wei, bookstore worker, 23

Ling, 8

The Moreno-Ryan family

Maya, 2

Ms. Ryan, office manager

Mr. Moreno, building contractor

Grandpa

Lauren, 10

Julian, 8

The Jacobs family

Mr. Jacobs, full-time dad

Ms. Jacobs, accountant

Ginny, 8

The Khan family

Ms. Khan, 5th grade teacher

Amir, 7

The Singh family

Dr. Singh, dentist

Mr. Singh, train conductor

Diya, 10

The Gorski-Feldstein family

Abigail, 3

Dr. Feldstein, pediatrician

Mr. Gorski, deli clerk

William, 7

The Clark family

Mr. Clark, firefighter

Ms. Clark, chef

Quincy, 11

Aunt Diane, architect

Joshua, 2

ceiling

Lauren opens the curtains
to let the sun shine
through the window.

curtain rod

curtains

window

hanger

closet

wall

dress

light
switch

yawning

pillow

bathrobe

bed

cat

alarm clock

glass

book

shirt

sheet

blanket

socks

Lauren is going to wear
her red jacket.
Where did she put it?

jacket

nightstand

floor

rug

hairbrush

piggy bank

bracelet

necklace

Good Morning!

Lauren and Julian wake up and
begin their morning routines.

Down the hall, Lauren's brother, Julian, brushes his teeth in the bathroom.

shade

mirror

tiles

rubber ducks

toothbrush

toothpaste

dental floss

shower

soap

tweezers

comb

nail clippers

lotion

sink

shower curtain

pajamas

towel

washcloth

toilet paper

step stool

Julian stands on a step stool to reach the sink.

toilet

plunger

shampoo

bath mat

conditioner

bathtub

Breakfast Time

The Moreno-Ryan family eats breakfast together in the kitchen.

refrigerator

freezer

window

cat

clock

bell pepper

cabbage

tomatoes

yogurt

milk

ice dispenser

faucet

sponge

sink

bagels

blender

cream cheese

juice

shopping list

dishwasher

cheese

fork

bacon

plate

carrots

broccoli

Lauren takes a bottle of juice from the refrigerator.

Grandpa helps Maya eat with a spoon.

high chair

spoon

glass

knife

bowl

garbage can

sippy cup

jam

cereal

nuts

saucepan

pot

beans

flour

rice

teapot

coffee pot

coffee

tongs

Julian makes toast by placing two slices of bread in the toaster.

spices

whisk

ladle

egg cups

tea bags

toast

plug

microwave

oil

sugar

electric kettle

bread

spatula

cooktop

toaster

oven

frying pan

dog

eggs

eating

oatmeal

Mr. Moreno cooks eggs in a frying pan on the cooktop. He flips them with a spatula.

table

mug

Ms. Ryan eats a nutritious bowl of oatmeal with berries and nuts on top.

flowers

pear

bananas

apple

pepper

salt

vase

fruit bowl

Getting Ready

The family gets ready to leave the house. Grandpa says goodbye to Lauren and Julian as they set off for school.

Mr. Moreno is ironing his shirt for work.

speaker

sofa

bookshelf

pillow

laundry basket

television

armchair

television remote

coffee table

iron

electrical outlet

ironing board

Maya plays tug-of-war with Prince, the family's pet dog.

watering can

chew toy

patio furniture

houseplant

Ms. Ryan waters the houseplants with a watering can.

tricycle

patio

birdhouse

tree

laundry

clothesline

squirrel

roof

bird feeder

door

bird

picture frame

fence

hose

soil

wheelbarrow

Lauren puts on her shoes and looks for her backpack. Where is it?

chair

jacket

shoe

Julian waves hello to his neighbor Ling, who lives next door. Ling is going to school, too.

hat

backpack

gate

waving

hedge

sock

rake

coat

footpath

weeds

lawn

lawn mower

paving stone

alphabet

a b c d e f g
h i j k l m n
o p q r s t u
v w x y z

shapes

circle

oval

square

hexagon

parallelogram

triangle

whiteboard

dry erase
marker

laptop

whiteboard eraser

folders

microscope

screen

desk

keyboard

binder

magnifying glass

teacher's
aide

worksheets

Julian looks for
Japan on the globe.

searching

The teacher's aide asks
William to help him
hand out worksheets.

globe

student

map

Welcome to Class

Julian and Ling are both students in Ms. Brown's second-grade class, where they learn math, science, language arts, and social studies.

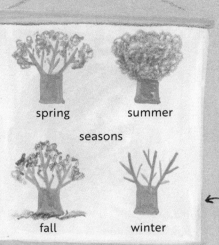

seasons

spring

summer

fall

winter

poster

calendar

teacher

bun

tablet

sweater

Amir raises his hand to ask Ms. Brown for help with his reading.

studying

textbook

Students study for an upcoming quiz by reading their textbooks.

Ginny uses a calculator to add numbers for a math problem.

pencil

pencil sharpener

concentrating

notebook

$9 + 7 = 16$
$11 + 5 = 16$
2

math

calculator

Let's Get Creative!

In Mr. Saleh's art class, students can try painting, drawing, collaging, and sculpting.

Mr. Saleh shows students how to mix blue and red to make purple.

Ling uses an easel to hold up her paper as she paints.

painting

sculpture

shelf

portrait

artwork

poster paint

palette

easel

paper

spilling

paintbrush

watercolor paint

Uh-oh! William spilled some green paint.

clay

yarn

string

black

pink

modeling tools

felt

brown

white

mobile

color wheel

orange   red

yellow

purple

green   blue

windowsill

drawing

crayons

pen   sketch

eraser

marker

sketchbook

apron

Julian needs the yellow crayon
to finish his picture.
Can you help him find it?

gluing

collage   glue

Ginny makes a collage by cutting
out pictures from magazines and
gluing them together.

scissors

colored
paper

glitter

19

Amazing Land Animals

The students in Ms. Khan's fifth-grade class are learning all about animals that live on land. The classroom display shows how animals are organized into groups based on things they have in common, such as whether they have fur, feathers, or scales.

Birds lay eggs and have feathers and one pair of legs.

NOT TO SCALE

nightingale

sparrow

emu

penguin

toucan

eagle

ostrich

hummingbird

flamingo

peacock

Amphibians such as frogs can survive both in water and on land.

crocodile

gecko

chameleon

toad

axolotl

alligator

salamander

iguana

tortoise

bullfrog

cobra

newt

Snakes, crocodiles, and lizards are all reptiles. They have scaly skin and most lay eggs.

Mammals have hair or fur and produce milk for their offspring. Humans are mammals, and so are elephants, tigers, and bears.

rhinoceros

sloth

tiger

cheetah

giant panda

kangaroo

porcupine

camel

monkey

hippopotamus

elephant

jaguar

bat

giraffe

zebra

lion

lemur

polar bear

butterfly

mosquito

praying mantis

grasshopper

bee

fly

ant

dragonfly

beetle

moth

Insects have three pairs of legs and a hard outer shell called an *exoskeleton*.

roof

sharing

toy horse

bookshelf

chess board

board game

marbles

spring toy

toy box

playhouse

yo-yo

toy train set

tunnel

jigsaw puzzle

stacking

Maya makes a tower out of building blocks.

dominos

laughing

puppet

blocks

ball

teddy bear

stuffed animal

Abigail and Joshua are having a tea party with dolls and stuffed animals.

teacup

saucer

pitcher

tea set

doll

action figure

Recess

During recess, some kids play inside with toys and others go outside to play games on the playground.

toy car

tree

swings

seesaw

tire swing

playing tag

hiding

monkey bars

The second graders are playing hide-and-seek on the playground. William is looking for Ling, Julian, and Amir. Do you see where they are hiding?

play structure

building

sandbox

crouching

slide

hoop

Some older girls are playing double Dutch by turning two jump ropes in opposite directions.

jumping

hopscotch

jump rope

cartwheel

Diya and Lauren have fun doing cartwheels and somersaults on the grass.

somersault

library

bulletin board

website

paper

computer

printer

mouse

mouse pad

bookshelf

Quincy uses a computer to look up information.

The librarian helps Lauren and her friend find the right books for their research project.

newspaper

magazine

magazine rack

Ms. Khan helps a student with their reading.

librarian

encyclopedia

reading

hijab

atlas

beanbag chair

bookmark

dictionary

lamp

Books and Cooks

Ms. Khan's class is going to the school library
while Ms. Brown's class has lunch in the cafeteria.

cafeteria

hairnet

cafeteria worker

broom

milk

recycling bin

juice boxes

hamburger

french fries

green beans

peas

Amir picks up his tray from
the lunch line and looks
for his friend Julian.
Can you find him?

tray

chopsticks

granola bar

bento box

potato chips

uniform

custodian

The custodian
uses a mop to
clean up a spill.

eating

Ginny brought a
sandwich and an
orange to school
in a lunch box.

pickle

paper bag

orange

sandwich

lunch box

mop

Almost Show Time...

Ms. Brown's class is getting ready for the talent show in the auditorium.

spotlight

songbook

recorder

A band is a group of people playing musical instruments together.

conductor

guitar

piano

flute

saxophone

clarinet

cello

amplifier

bow

violin

conductor's baton

wire

cymbals

Julian uses a script to practice his lines. A script includes all the words in a stage play.

rehearsing

baseball cap

drums

director

script

trumpet

trumpet case

The director instructs actors on how to perform their lines.

megaphone

wheelchair

In the choir, a group of
singers practices a new song.

curtain

singing

choir

audience

overalls

music stand

William is excited to sing
a solo all by himself.

Ling and Ginny have fun
trying on costumes for
their performance.

microphone

soloist

sheet music

costume

bowler hat

dancing

pirouette

tie

tutu

The dancers wear
different kinds
of shoes to dance
ballet, tap, or jazz.

jazz
shoes

tap shoes

ballet
shoes

27

Go, Team!

After school, students rush to the field to play their favorite sports.

Lauren puts on her jersey and cleats to practice with the soccer team.

soccer field

tackling

jersey

goal

referee

cleats

kicking

soccer ball

goalie

goalpost

stretching

sweating

athlete

hurdle

running

Quincy takes the baton from another runner in the relay and runs the last lap.

jumping jacks

baton

track

Some kids prefer to watch and cheer for their friends from the sidelines.

flag

cheering

fans

sidelines

Diya is the captain of the basketball team. She leads the other players and keeps them focused.

basketball hoop

scoreboard

basketball

reaching

throwing

captain

5 2

field

basketball court

teammates

shorts

sit-up

whistle

The coach is about to blow the whistle to tell the players that the game is half over.

push-up

coach

stopwatch

Substitute players stretch and do exercises to keep warm while they wait for their turns to play.

net

tennis ball

tennis court

racket

water bottle

duffel bag

The ocean is home to trillions of fish, as well as other types of animals including mammals and even some reptiles, such as sea turtles.

sea lion

seal

angelfish

cuttlefish

walrus

A group of fish swimming together is called a *school*.

stingray

starfish

seahorses

parrotfish

octopus

crab

clownfish

sea sponge

lionfish

clam

pufferfish

sea urchin

sea anemone

lobster

Under the Sea

Did you know that water covers most of the Earth's surface? The ocean is very large and teeming with life. Diya has a poster on her bedroom wall showing many different types of creatures that live underwater.

sea turtle

Whales and dolphins are mammals.
They breathe air using a nostril on top
of their heads called a *blowhole*.

dolphin

orca

barnacles

barracuda

whale

manatee

tail

fin

gills

jellyfish

sea snake

shark

squid

Sharks, like other fish,
take in oxygen from
the water using special
organs called *gills*.

anglerfish

tentacle

tuna

31

hotel

movie theater

salon

post office

streetlight

Mr. Gorski is getting a haircut and a shave at the barbershop.

clothing store

mail carrier

barber

mail bag

mail

crossing guard

stop sign

curb

bus

The crossing guard directs traffic to keep pedestrians safe.

crosswalk

ice cream truck

wheelchair

turban

street

baker

pedestrian

trash can

apron

sidewalk

stroller

A Busy City Street

A city street is a lively place with many kinds of shops and businesses.

roof garden

art gallery

cat

café

bakery

Wei parks his bicycle outside the bookstore.

toy store

Ms. Clark picks up medicine from the pharmacy.

butcher

bookstore

bus stop

pharmacy

ham

bicycle

cycling

bike lane

manhole cover

traffic light

truck

car

taxi

dog walker

fruit stand

dogs

A Trip to the Doctor

There are many kinds of doctors who help us keep our bodies healthy.

skeleton

thermometer

blood pressure cuff

cotton pads

doctor

listening

lab coat

stethoscope

scale

Dr. Feldstein uses a stethoscope to hear the patient's heartbeat.

waiting room

cast

receptionist

crutches

medical scrubs

nurse

sneezing

A nurse asks a patient in the waiting room to answer a questionnaire.

bandage

clipboard

coughing

Ling and her grandma check in at the reception desk.

eye

iris

pupil

E
F P
T Q Z
L F E D I H
D E F P O T E C

optometrist

scarf

suit

glasses

autorefractor

form

The optometrist gives
Ginny an eye test to check
if she needs glasses.

X-ray

dentist

Dr. Singh is checking
Quincy's teeth for small
holes, or cavities.

mask

latex
gloves

braces

dental
hygienist

tattoo

dental tools

dentist's
chair

kiwi
plum
pear
strawberry
blackberry
blueberries
raspberry
mango
watermelon

dairy
butter
frozen foods
yogurt
margarine
sour cream
waffles
pizza
ice cream
peas
corn
pointing
zucchini

customer
cauliflower
asparagus

Ginny asks her mom if they can buy ice cream in the frozen foods section.

Mr. Gorski prepares meat and cheese for customers at the deli counter.

deli

shopping list

Ms. Khan uses a shopping list to remember what she needs to buy. Can you help her find the bananas?

cheese
salami
sausages
Swiss cheese

Grocery Shopping

People buy food from the grocery store to make into meals at home.

cherries

milk

shelf

chocolate milk

pushing

cucumber

cart

At the cash register, a customer pays with a credit card and the cashier gives her a receipt.

cashier

receipt

credit card

conveyor belt

bag

grapefruit · lemons · limes

squash

green grapes

pumpkin

apple

red grapes

bananas

sweet potatoes

onion

potatoes

peaches

garlic

mushrooms

kale

basket

celery

A customer is shopping for fresh fruits and vegetables in the produce section.

cash register

coins

papaya

bills

baguette

cantaloupe

crackers

pasta

canned soup

hot sauce

mustard

ketchup

taco shells

dried beans

gazebo

kite

wall

entrance

grass

statue

The Clark and Moreno-Ryan families are meeting up for a picnic at the picnic tables.

Quincy and Aunt Diane unpack food from a picnic basket.

lemonade

picnic table

scooter

picnic basket

camera

A photographer uses a camera to take pictures of the local wildlife.

headphones

runner

bench

T-shirt

photographer

musician

The musician plays songs for the people passing by.

wicket

At the Park

A park is the perfect place to relax, play, and enjoy the outdoors with friends and family.

croquet mallet

croquet ball

ramp

skateboard

skating

helmet

knee pads

roller skates

flowers

fountain

swan

pond

branch

bird

chicks

nest

path

goose

dog

rowboat

oar

frog

lily pad

lily

binoculars

reeds

Ling and her grandma go birdwatching using binoculars. They are looking for a red bird with its nest. Can you tell them where to look?

birdwatching

duck

duckling

39

spaghetti

grilled cheese

booth

A diner asks the waiter which meals are vegetarian because he does not eat any meat.

meatballs

salad   lasagna

tablecloth

waiter

balloon

The host welcomes diners to the restaurant and brings menus to their table.

candles

table

pizza

birthday cake

gift

host

Ling gives a gift to her big brother. Happy birthday, Wei!

diner

napkin

A Special Dinner

The Chen family is celebrating Wei's birthday at a restaurant.

steamer

french fries

ramen

Ms. Clark, the head chef, directs the other cooks in the kitchen.

fryer

hot burner

chef's hat

busser

dishes

chef

sushi

cook

slicing

steak

tagine

sprinkling

biryani

Mr. Saleh and his friends eat appetizers before their main courses arrive.

sausages

lobster

samosas

soup

taco

shrimp

salsa

dinner rolls

butter

dumplings

chicken fingers

Under Construction

Mr. Moreno and his team are building a new apartment building using tools and powerful machines.

lifting

bricks

dump truck

cab

backhoe

crane

crane operator

bulldozer

blade

cement mixer

lumber

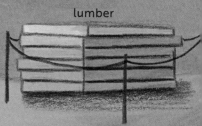

building contractor

clipboard

digging

cone

shovel

Mr. Moreno, the building contractor, manages a team of workers and makes sure everything goes smoothly.

pipe
hammer
plumber
wrench
level
measuring tape

Architects draw plans called blueprints that show the workers what to do.

architect
blueprint
builder

paint roller
paintbrush
paint
painter
ladder

scaffolding

pliers
ruler
nail
safety glasses
stairs
hard hat
drill
cabinet
saw
screwdriver

Safety is always important on a work site! Everybody wears hard hats and other protective gear.

construction worker

concrete

A worker puts up caution tape to keep people from walking on the wet concrete.

caution tape

wheelbarrow

43

fire station

police station

road

van

siren

police car

ambulance

wheel

fire engine

radio

police officer

stretcher

paramedic

Paramedics wait nearby with an ambulance to get people to a hospital if needed.

Emergency!

Firefighters and other emergency workers hurry to help when there is trouble!

44

Mr. Clark is a firefighter. He climbs a ladder to rescue people trapped in the building.

climbing

smoke

fire

rung

ladder

water

fire hydrant

Firefighters wear helmets, gloves, boots, and heavy clothes to protect themselves.

firefighter

boots

fire hose

A big hose with water is sprayed at the fire to extinguish the flames.

45

Julian and Lauren look down over the fairground from the Ferris wheel.

Ferris wheel

beekeeper

honey

jam

juggling

judging

pie

Swiss roll

cupcakes

A juggler entertains the crowd with a juggling act.

juggler

Dr. Feldstein buys honey from the beekeeper's stand.

beanbag toss

cake

cookies

A group of judges decides which cakes and pies will win the baking competition.

sheep

pig

lamb

piglet

ring toss

goat

kid

horse

three-legged race

rabbit

Explore the Fair

Visitors to the fair can go on rides, see farm animals, enjoy performances, and play games.

fun house

balloons

bumper cars

candy apple

donuts

lollipop

A judge gives Ms. Clark a blue ribbon. Her quilt won first prize in the arts and crafts contest!

quilt

unicorn

cotton candy

candy cane

pretzel

hot dog

blue ribbon

merry-go-round

llama

The mother cow licks the head of her calf, who is just learning how to walk.

rooster

calf

cow

farmer

foal

Somebody left the gate open at the chicken coop! Can you find all five missing chickens?

chicken

Splish Splash!

Some people like to stay indoors and keep dry when it rains. But there's plenty to do and see outside on a rainy day.

rainbow

cloud

leash

stick

dog

dog collar

mud

The rain soaks into the soil and helps the flowers grow.

crocuses

duck

pond

ripples

diving

umbrella

egg   robin

The robin sits on its nest to protect its eggs from the rain.

gutter

moss

awning

Ms. Brown waits under a store awning to keep dry.

daffodil

drainpipe

drain

plant pot

hood

rain

raincoat

Someone has snuck off with Ginny's lunch box! Can you help her find it?

boots

Diya makes a paper boat and watches it float in a puddle.

daisies

tulip

puddle

The souvenir shop sells T-shirts, beach toys, and other items so visitors can remember their beach days.

ice cream

volleyball

ice pop

snow cone

cane

seagull

fan

sandals

Mr. Moreno inflates a beach ball by blowing air into it.

sunglasses

one-piece swimsuit

Lauren is helping Maya build a sandcastle.

sandcastle

sunburn

beach ball

bucket

wetsuit

towel

seashell

shovel

crab

By the Seaside

When the weather is hot, it's fun to cool off by taking a trip to the beach.

palm tree

dune

net

beach umbrella

lifeguard

sun hat

sunscreen

sand

Ling's grandma puts on sunscreen and wears a sun hat to protect her skin from the sun.

floating

flip-flops

goggles

visor

bikini

swim trunks

splashing

Julian and Ling splash in the waves.

swimming

chimney

Mr. Clark shovels snow from the sidewalk while Ms. Clark spreads salt to melt the slippery ice.

snow bank

toboggan

snowblower

shovel

mittens

vest

snow pants

wool hat

thermos

snowshoes

William tries to catch a snowflake on his tongue.

icicle

snow angel

snowball

snow boots

sled

snowman

Quincy is bundled up in a warm coat, snow pants, mittens, and a wool hat so he can play in the snow.

A Snowy Day

Snow covers the ground in a cold, wet, sparkly white layer.

snowplow

hill

The cars in the street turn the white snow into gray slush.

horse

sleigh

car

salt truck

ski poles

skis

snow

slush

earmuffs

ice

hockey stick

puck

hockey skates

figure skating

scarf

figure skates

gloves

The water in the pond has frozen hard enough that people can skate on the ice.

timetable

airport

baggage counter

suitcase

The airport security team uses X-ray scanners to check for liquids, sharp objects, or anything else that could be dangerous on a flight.

baggage scanner

metal detector

security officer

The Gorski family is checking their suitcases at the baggage counter before they go through security.

A train track is made of many rails joined together.

rail

freight train

17806

Passenger trains carry people and freight trains carry cargo, such as food or building materials.

passenger train

Safe Travels!

There are many ways to travel from place to place. Would you rather travel up high in an airplane, or over the ground on a train?

control
tower

takeoff

landing

runway

flight attendant

boarding gate

18

airplane

passenger

tarmac

boarding pass

Ms. Chen is a pilot.
She flies the airplane
and her copilot
helps her.

briefcase

copilot

pilot

train station

ticket
machine

ticket counter

turnstile

train
conductor

driver

porter

train track

owl

camper

awning

hammock

fireflies

grill

tent

rabbits

Diya and her dad
work together to pitch
a tent to sleep in.

lantern

sleeping bag

Amir toasts
marshmallows
over the fire.

marshmallows

log

deer

axe

cooler

mouse

firewood

campfire

Camping Adventure

Camping is a fun way to spend time in
nature and take a break from everyday life.

badger

hawk

sunset

cabin

fox

snake

squirrel

visitor center

hiking

Mr. Saleh stays on the trails to avoid disturbing the plants and wildlife.

hedgehog

paddle

dock

The dock has different kinds of boats that people can rent.

park ranger

flashlight

beaver

rowboat

canoe

paddleboat

twig

pine cone

Campers put on bug spray to keep away mosquitoes.

bug spray

The park ranger teaches campers about the plants and animals of the forest.

Index

Meet the Author and Illustrator

Hannah Campbell is a writer, editor, and lifelong word nerd. Her favorite parts of this book are the city street and park scenes because she loves seeing all the ways that people can gather and have fun together. She enjoys running, riding her bike, sewing clothes, and singing. Hannah has written several children's activity books, including some based on the works of Roald Dahl. She grew up in Dearborn, Michigan, and now lives in Queens, New York, with her husband and cat. This book is dedicated to her nephew, Will, who is learning new words every day.

Sara Rhys is an illustrator based in a small town in the Scottish Borders in the UK. She holds a degree in Contemporary Applied Arts and previously worked as a metalsmith before turning her skills to illustration. Sara creates her artworks by hand using watercolors, gouache, and colored pencils, finished with a bit of digital magic. Her first illustrated children's book, *Pony Poems for Little Pony Lovers*, was published in 2019. Sara loved illustrating the camping scene in this book because it shows people appreciating nature and combines some of her favorite things to draw—wildlife and trees. When she's not working, Sara likes gardening, walking by the sea, spending time with her friends, and cooking vegan food.

Merriam-Webster Kids is an imprint of Merriam-Webster Inc., published in collaboration with What on Earth Publishing.

First published in the United States in 2022

Developed by What on Earth Publishing

Written by Hannah Campbell
Illustrated by Sara Rhys
Designed by Daisy Symes
Edited by Max Bisantz and Meg Osborne
Indexed by Connie Binder
Print and Production Consultancy by Booklabs.co.uk

Merriam-Webster Inc.: Patty Sullivan, Publisher; Linda Wood, Senior Editor; Em Vezina, Director of Editorial Operations

What on Earth Publishing: Nancy Feresten, Publisher; Natalie Bellos, Editorial Director; Max Bisantz, Executive Editor; Meg Osborne, Assistant Editor; Andy Forshaw, Art Director; Daisy Symes, Designer

Library of Congress Cataloging-in-Publication Data available upon request
First Edition, 2022

ISBN: 9780877791249

Printed in Canada

TC/Quebec, Canada/06/2022